Making a Difference on VACATION

by Hermione Redshaw

Minneapolis, Minnesota

Credits: All images courtesy of Shutterstock.com. With thanks to Getty Images, Thinkstock Photo, and iStockphoto. Recurring images © Weshitelist (font), AnastasiaNi (background pattern), GoodStudio (vectors). Cover © Oleh Svetiukha, GoodStudio. 2&3 © Oleh Svetiukha. 4&5 © Pavel L Photo and Video, pixelheadphoto digitalskillet, vectortatu. 6&7 © Iryna Dincer, Yuganov Konstantin. 8&9 © Monkey Business Images, KarepaStock. 10&11 © Monkey Business Images, wavebreakmedia. 12&13 © Monkey Business Images, New Africa. 14&15 © Syda Productions, LordRunar. 16&17 © Lucky Business, pakul54. 18&19 © GOLFX, Flamingo Images, Igoror. 20&21 © Onzeg, fizkes, VectorSun58. 22&23 © DGLimages, RichVintage.

Library of Congress Cataloging-in-Publication Data is available at www.loc.gov or upon request from the publisher.

ISBN: 979-8-88509-360-6 (hardcover)
ISBN: 979-8-88509-482-5 (paperback)
ISBN: 979-8-88509-597-6 (ebook)

© 2023 Booklife Publishing
This edition is published by arrangement with Booklife Publishing.

North American adaptations © 2023 Bearport Publishing Company. All rights reserved. No part of this publication may be reproduced in whole or in part, stored in any retrieval system, or transmitted in any form or by any means, electronic, mechanical, photocopying, recording, or otherwise, without written permission from the publisher.

For more information, write to Bearport Publishing, 5357 Penn Avenue South, Minneapolis, MN 55419.

CONTENTS

Time for a Vacation!........... 4
Out and About................. 6
Rent to Reuse 8
Keep It Clean 10
Why Recycle?................. 12
Protect Wildlife 14
Learn about Animals.......... 16
Save Energy! 18
Try Meat-Free Meals 20
Staycations 22
Glossary 24
Index 24

TIME FOR A VACATION!

Going on vacation is a time to relax and have fun. But you can still do things to help our **planet**! Earth is our shared home, and we must take care of it.

Wherever you travel, you can make a difference. Let's go save the world on vacation!

Earth is home to about 8 billion people.

OUT AND ABOUT

How should you get around to explore your vacation spot? Cars are bad for Earth because they cause **pollution**. You can help by walking instead of driving.

Taking buses and trains helps, too. They carry many people at once. This makes less pollution because there are not as many cars.

Many big cities have underground trains called subways to help people get around.

RENT TO REUSE

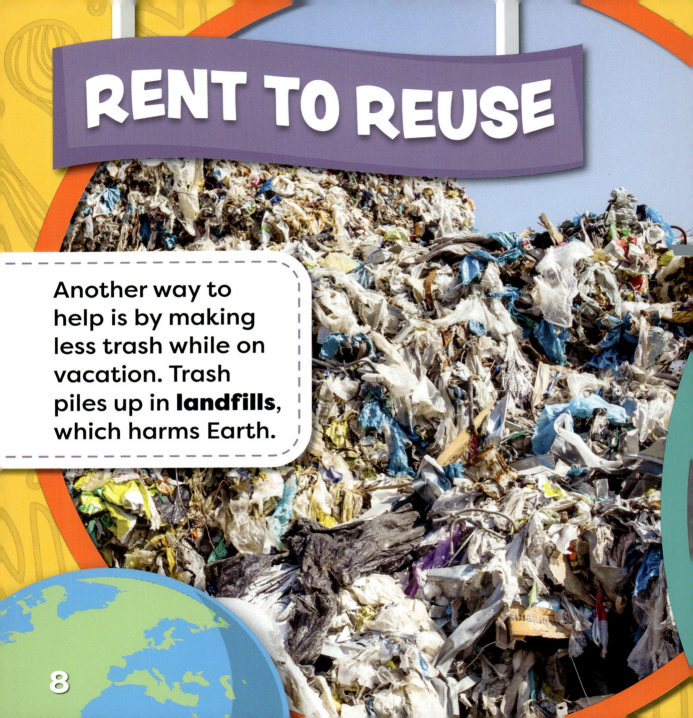

Another way to help is by making less trash while on vacation. Trash piles up in **landfills**, which harms Earth.

How can you make less trash? **Reuse** things when you can. You could rent reusable things such as bodyboards for your vacation activities.

Rented items get reused by many people.

KEEP IT CLEAN

Bring reusable items from home, too. You can pack reusable plates and cups for when you eat on vacation.

If there is something you can't reuse, be smart about how you get rid of it. Make sure you do not **litter**. We want our planet to be clean, so we should not leave trash on the ground.

WHY RECYCLE?

One of the best ways to get rid of things is to **recycle** them when you can. Items that go in recycling bins will be made into new things. This helps the planet.

Many paper, plastic, glass, and metal items can be recycled.

Keep your eye out for recycling bins while you're on vacation!

PROTECT WILDLIFE

If you explore outdoors on vacation, be sure to stick to the paths. This helps keep the land around you safe for plants and animals.

For a camping trip, find a clear space to pitch your tent. Keep any grills or stoves away from plants so you don't accidentally start a fire.

Remember to clean up after yourself. Leave the area as you found it.

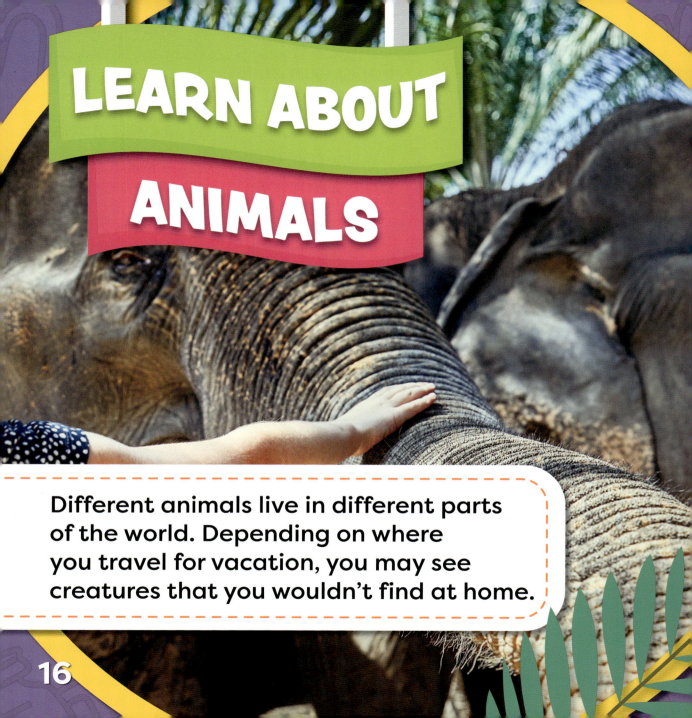

LEARN ABOUT ANIMALS

Different animals live in different parts of the world. Depending on where you travel for vacation, you may see creatures that you wouldn't find at home.

A safe way to learn about wildlife is by visiting animal **sanctuaries**. These places work to protect animals.

What kinds of animals will you see on vacation? You could look for . . .

- A scaly creature
- A big cat
- Something with a shell
- A colorful bird
- A small insect

SAVE ENERGY!

Energy powers lamps, heaters, and more. But using too much energy can harm the planet. That's why it's important to save energy, even on vacation!

Remember to turn off lights when you leave a room and unplug things when you are done using them. Keep your hot showers short, too.

TRY MEAT-FREE MEALS

Vacations are a great time to try new things! Why not try a meat-free meal? Farming lots of animals for meat can be bad for the planet. Eating less meat will help.

You can look on restaurant menus for meals labeled **vegetarian**. This means the food does not have any meat.

There are even some foods, such as veggie burgers, that look like meat but are made from plants.

STAYCATIONS

If you can't travel for vacation, you can still have fun close to home. It's called a staycation!

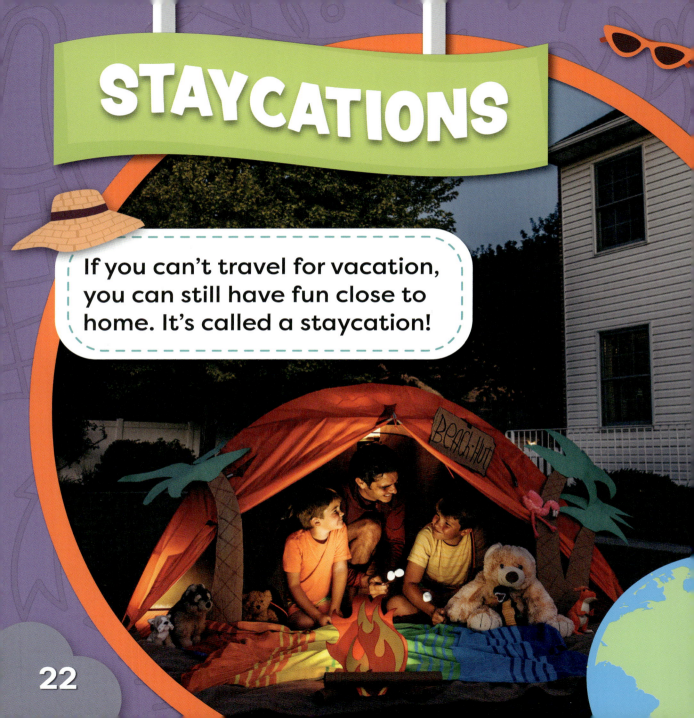

Staycations help the planet because you don't fly or drive anywhere. This means less pollution from airplanes and cars.

For your staycation, you could play in a park near your home or stay inside and watch your favorite movies.

GLOSSARY

landfills large holes in the ground used for dumping trash

litter trash that has been left on the ground

planet a large, round object that circles the sun

pollution harmful things being added to nature

recycle to turn used, unwanted things into new, useful things

reuse to use again

sanctuaries places where animals are protected

vegetarian having no meat

INDEX

airplanes 23
animals 14, 16–17, 20
energy 18
plants 14–15, 21
plastic 13
pollution 6–8, 23
staycations 22–23
tent 15
vegetarian 21